SUPER SANDCASTLE™
It's the Alphabet!

# It's L!

## Oona Gaarder-Juntti

Consulting Editor, Diane Craig, M.A./Reading Specialist

ABDO
Publishing Company

Published by ABDO Publishing Company, 8000 West 78th Street, Edina, Minnesota 55439. Copyright © 2010 by Abdo Consulting Group, Inc. International copyrights reserved in all countries. No part of this book may be reproduced in any form without written permission from the publisher. Super SandCastle™ is a trademark and logo of ABDO Publishing Company.

Printed in the United States.

♺ PRINTED ON RECYCLED PAPER

Editor: Liz Salzmann
Content Developer: Nancy Tuminelly
Cover and Interior Design and Production: Kelly Doudna, Mighty Media
Photo Credits: iStockphoto (Jani Bryson), Shutterstock

**Library of Congress Cataloging-in-Publication Data**
Gaarder-Juntti, Oona, 1979-
  It's L! / Oona Gaarder-Juntti.
     p. cm. -- (It's the Alphabet!)
  ISBN 978-1-60453-599-0
  1. English language--Alphabet--Juvenile literature. 2. Alphabet books--Juvenile literature. I. Title.
  PE1155.G2936 2010
  421'.1--dc22
  〈E〉
                                        2009021007

Super SandCastle™ books are created by a team of professional educators, reading specialists, and content developers around five essential components— phonemic awareness, phonics, vocabulary, text comprehension, and fluency—to assist young readers as they develop reading skills and strategies and increase their general knowledge. All books are written, reviewed, and leveled for guided reading, early reading intervention, and Accelerated Reader® programs for use in shared, guided, and independent reading and writing activities to support a balanced approach to literacy instruction.

## About SUPER SANDCASTLE™

**Bigger Books for Emerging Readers**
**Grades K–4**

Created for library, classroom, and at-home use, Super SandCastle™ books support and engage young readers as they develop and build literacy skills and will increase their general knowledge about the world around them. Super SandCastle™ books are an extension of SandCastle™, the leading preK–3 imprint for emerging and beginning readers. Super SandCastle™ features a larger trim size for more reading fun.

**Let Us Know**
Super SandCastle™ would like to hear your stories about reading this book. What was your favorite page? Was there something hard that you needed help with? Share the ups and downs of learning to read. We want to hear from you! Send us an e-mail.

sandcastle@abdopublishing.com

Contact us for a complete list of SandCastle™, Super SandCastle™, and other nonfiction and fiction titles from ABDO Publishing Company.

www.abdopublishing.com • 8000 West 78th Street
Edina, MN 55439 • 800-800-1312 • 952-831-1632 fax

Aa Bb Cc Dd Ee
Ff Gg Hh Ii Jj Kk
Ll Mm Nn Oo Pp
Qq Rr Ss Tt Uu Vv
Ww Xx Yy Zz

# The Letter Ll

The letter **l** in American Sign Language

**L** and **l** can also look like

Ll   Ll

Ll   Ll

Ll   Ll

4

The letter l is a consonant.

It is the 12th letter of the alphabet.

☞ Some words start with l.

ladybug

log

# Lauren

Lauren looks at a large ladybug lying on a log.

☞ Some words have **l** in the middle.

**butterf**l**y**

**f**l**ower**

Sometimes a middle l is silent.

Claire could see the black and gold butterfly walk alone on a blue flower.

9

Some words have **l** at the end.

pencil

snail

Paul can feel the snail crawl on his hand until it reaches the pencil.

Paul

11

Some words have a double l.

doll

wall

Ella's small doll and yellow ball fell off a really tall wall.

ball

☞ In Spanish words, the double l sounds like **y**.

quesadilla

Guillermo uses tortillas to make quesadillas in La Jolla.

tortilla

Lucy is a little ladybug
that likes to climb and fly.

She lands on yellow flowers
and loves the large blue sky.

Lucy is always friendly to the butterflies and beetles she sees.

She is polite and usually says, "Will you excuse me, please?"

Lucy doesn't have black circles
and that makes her feel really blue.

All the snails laugh and say,
"What kind of silly ladybug are you?"

The following day Lucy glues
black pebbles all over her shell.

They looked swell until she flapped
her wings and off the pebbles fell.

She talks with Larry the caterpillar and asks what she should do.

Larry listens closely to Lucy as she tells him all about the glue.

Larry tells her that she looks lovely and is really clever too.

Lucy is thrilled and happily exclaims, "Larry, you're a good friend, it's true!"

Which words have
the letter l?

## ladybug

## flower

## car

## caterpillar

house

tortilla

goose

snail

# Glossary

**clever** (p. 20) – able to learn things quickly.

**double** (pp. 12, 13) – two of the same thing.

**exclaim** (p. 20) – to speak with strong feeling.

**flap** (p. 18) – to move up and down or back and forth.

**pebble** (p. 18) – a small rock or stone.

**polite** (p. 16) – having good manners or showing consideration for others.

**quesadilla** (p. 13) – a dish with cheese and sometimes vegetables and meat melted between two tortillas.

**thrill** (p. 20) – to make someone feel very excited or happy.

**tortilla** (pp. 13, 23) – a flat, round bread made from either corn or wheat flour.

**usually** (p. 16) – commonly or normally.

To promote letter recognition, letters are highlighted instead of glossary words in this series. The page numbers above indicate where the glossary words can be found.

## More Words with L

Find the l in the beginning, middle, or end of each word.

| | | | | |
|---|---|---|---|---|
| animal | girl | late | lose | owl |
| bell | glad | leg | loss | rule |
| bull | lamb | let | lost | sleep |
| cold | lamp | light | lot | turtle |
| elephant | lap | line | low | uphill |
| family | last | lion | oil | walk |